# *This Gift Belongs*

*to...*

_____

*From:*

_____

*Date:*

_____

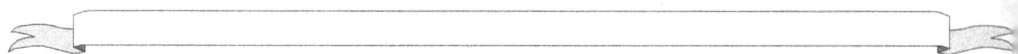

ANOINTED

# *PRAYERS*

## GOING DEEP
## 40 DAYS 40 NIGHTS OF PRAYER

~~~~~~~~~~PRAYER JOURNAL~~~~~~~~~~

### A.M. PRAYERS

Sis.Lynn Ingram

Edited by: Minister, Carla Carrington

Cover Design: SOS Graphic Designs

Published by G Publishing, LLC

Library of Congress Control Number:  2017904070

ISBN: 978-0-9987663-1-7

Printed in the United States of America

*Before praying, make a list of people and things you want to pray for. This will help you keep focus.*

*Find a place where there are no distractions. A quiet place. A place for you and God.*

*When you start the Prayer Journal, complete the first a.m. prayer in the morning. In the evening, flip the book to the p.m. prayers and complete the first p.m. prayer. Repeat this process until you have completed 40 days (a.m. prayers) and 40 nights (p.m. prayers).*

Let the words of my mouth and the mediation of my heart, be acceptable in thy sight O LORD, My strength, and my redeemer. ~ Psalms 19: 4

*I believe, as you journal your prayers these 40 Days 40 nights. There's going to be a great transformation in your life. and manifestation of your gifts. As you sit and meditate on God in your quiet time. I believe God is going to do a new thing in you.*

*And be not conformed to this world: But be ye transformed by the renewing of your mind, that ye may prove what is that good, and acceptable, and perfect, will of God.*
*Romans 12:2 ~KJV*

*"If you ask anything in My name, I will do it."*
*John 14:14 ~NKJV*

*For "whoever calls on the name of the LORD shall be saved.*
*Romans 10:13 ~NKJV*

*My prayer is... That the same the anointing on the words in this Journal will bless your life. And that you receive a greater relationship with Jesus, the presence of God in all you do. And give you a will to pray daily and to meditate on His Word.*

## *"My Confession"*

*Lord God I confess JESUS CHRIST as my personal savior. I believe he died on the cross for my sins, and rose from the dead. And now in heaven seated at the right hand of God making intercession on my behalf.*

**If you confess with your mouth that Jesus is Lord and believe in your heart that God raised him from the dead, you will be saved. *~Romans 10:9***

**For it is written: As I live, saith the Lord, every knee shall bow to me, and every toung shall comfess to God. *~Romans 14:11***

### *"Father forgive me, for I have sinned"*

*Lord, I come boldly to your throne of grace. asking for your forgiveness. Father God please forgive me of my sin, knowing and unknowing!*
*Lord, I'm saying I have sinned and done evil in your sight, forgive me O' Lord wash me and I shall be clean. This is my request for forgivness!*

*I thank you for your forgiving me of my sin. In the precious name of Jesus Christ, Amen.*

**For sin  shall not have dominion over you: for ye are not under the law, but under grace.**
**~ Romans 6:14 KJV**

**For all have sinned and fall short of the glory of God, ~Romans 3:23 ~NIV**

**"If we confess our sins, he is faithful and just to forgive us our sin and to cleanse us from all unrighteousness. ~I John1:9 ~KJV**

**"I, even I, am He who blots out your transgressions for My own sake: and I will not remember your sin. Isaiah 43:25 ~NKJV**

*Before I enter this 40 Days 40 Nights Journal I must worship you God, I invite you in my heart. Take resident in me. Fill me with your presence, fill me with your Spirit, fill me with your love. My desire is to be more like you Father. You're so great and kind. Gracious and merciful, mighty God you are! I love you and I adore you. There's none like you.*

*You are... El Shaddai~The Almighty God*
*You are... Jehovah Nissi ~ My Banner*
*You are... Jehovah Tsidkenu ~ My Righteousness*
*You are... Jehovah Rapha ~ My Healer*
*You are... Jehovah Jireh ~ My Provider*
*You are... Jehovah Shalom ~ My Peace*

*You are my everything, And God I say thank you, I bless you, I lift my hands to you in worship, I bow down before you, I enthrone you, I adore you, I praise you for who you are. You are God and God alone. The earth is yours and the fullness there of the world and a they that dwell therein! God I thank you for your presence right now, I bless your Holy name. in the precious name of Jesus AND IT IS SO.*

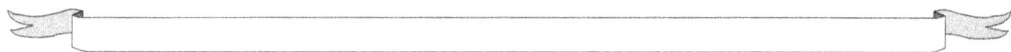

"THE PRAYER GATES ARE OPEN"


YOU MAY ENTER...

*O taste and see that the Lord is good: Blessed is the man who takes refuge in Him! ~Psalm 34:8 KJV*

*In peace, I will lie down and sleep, for you alone, O LORD, will keep me safe.* ~Psalm 4:8 NLT

_____

_____

_____

_____

_____

_____

_____

_____

_____

_____

_____

_____

_____

_____

_____

*Give us this day our daily bread.*
*~Matthew 6:11 KJV*

*Search me, O God and know my heart: try me, and know my thoughts: Psalm 139:23 KJV*

we walk by faith, not by sight.
~2 Corinthians 5:7 KJV

*And my God will meet all your needs according to the riches of his glory in Christ Jesus.*
*~Phillippians 4:19 NIV*

*Seek ye the LORD while he may be found, call ye upon him while he is near: ~ Isaiah 55:6 KJV*

And he said unto me, my grace is sufficient for thee: for my strength is made perfect in weakness. most gladly therefore will I rather glory in my infirmities, that the power of Christ may rest upon me. ~II Corinthians 12: 9 KJV

*Thou will show me the path of life: in thy presence is fullness of joy; at thy right hand, there are pleasure forevermore. ~Psalm 16:11 KJV*

_____

_____

_____

_____

_____

_____

_____

_____

_____

_____

_____

_____

_____

*He maketh me to lie down in green pastures; he leadeth me beside the still waters.* ~Psalm 23:2 KJV

_____

_____

_____

_____

_____

_____

_____

_____

_____

_____

_____

_____

_____

_____

_____

_____

*Trust in the LORD with all thine heart, and lean not unto thine own understanding.  ~Proverbs 3:5 KJV*

But they that wait upon the LORD shall renew their strength; they shall mount up with wings as eagles; they shall run, and not be weary; and they shall walk, and not faint.   Isaiah 40:31 KJV

---

---

---

---

---

---

---

---

---

---

---

---

---

*Put on the full armor of God of that ye may be able to stand against the wiles of the devil.*
*~Ephesians 6:11 KJV*

_____

_____

_____

_____

_____

_____

_____

_____

_____

_____

_____

_____

_____

*Abide in me and I in you, as the branch cannot bear fruit of itself, except it abide in the vine; no more can ye except, ye abide in me.  ~John 15:5 KJV*

_____

_____

_____

_____

_____

_____

_____

_____

_____

_____

_____

_____

_____

_____

_____

_____

## "HELP... Lord I messed up!"

1. have mercy upon me Oh God, according to Thy loving kindness; according unto the multitude of Thy tender mercies, blot out my transgressions.
2. Wash me thoroughly from mine iniquity, and cleanse me from my sin.
3. For I acknowledge my transgressions, and my sin is ever before me.
4. Against Thee, thee only, have I sinned and done this evil in thy sight: that thou mightest be justified when thou speakest, and be clear when thou judgest.
5. Behold, I was shapen in iniquity; and in sin did my mother conceive me.
6. Behold, thou desirest truth in the inward parts: and in the hidden part thou shalt make me to know wisdom.
7. Purge me with hyssop, and I shall be clean: wash me, and I shall be whiter than snow.

8. Make me to hear joy and gladness; that the bones which thou hast broken may rejoice.

9. Hide thy face from my sins, and blot out all mine iniquities.

10. Create in me a clean heart, O God; and renew a right spirit within me.

Psalm 51: 1-10 ~KJV

Many are the afflictions of the righteous: but the Lord delivereth him out of them all.  ~Psalm 34:19

*For God hath not given us the spirit of fea; but pf power, and love, and of a sound mind II Timothy 1: 7 KJV*

_____

_____

_____

_____

_____

_____

_____

_____

_____

_____

_____

_____

_____

*...The LORD is with you while you are with Him. If you seek Him, He will be found by you; but if you forsake Him, He will forsake you. ~ 2 Chronicles 15: 2b NKJV*

*Teach me, O LORD, the way of your statutes, and I shall keep it to the end. ~Psalm 119:33 NKJV*

Blessed is the man that walketh not in the counsel of the ungodly, nor standeth in the way of sinners, nor sitteth in the seat of the scornful. ~Psalm 1: 1 KJV

But you belong to God, my dear children. You have already won a victory over those people, because the Spirit who lives in you is greater than the spirit who lives in the world. ~ John 4:4 NLT

*Let your conversation be gracious and attractive so that you will have the right response for everyone.*
*~Colossians 4:6 NLT*

Don't Worry about anything: instead, pray about everything. Tell God what you need, and thank him for all he has done. ~Philippians 4:6 NLT

*Jabez cried out to the God of Israel, "Oh, that you would bless me and enlarge my territory! Let your hand be with me, and keep me from harm so that I will be free from pain." And God granted his request.*
*~ 1 Chronicles 4:10 NIV*

For it is by grace you have been saved, through faith –
and this is not from yourselves, it is the gift of God–
~Ephesians 2:8 NIV

Jesus Christ the same yesterday, and today, and forever.  ~Hebrews 13:8 KJV

The blessing of the LORD, it maketh rich, and he addeth no sorrow with it. ~Proverbs 10:22 KJV

*But seek ye first the kingdom of God, and his righteousness; and all these things shall be added unto you.  ~Matthew 6:33~KJV*

*Godly sorrow brings repentance that leads to salvation and leaves no regret, but worldly sorrow brings death.*
*~ II Corinthians 7:10 NIV*

_____

_____

_____

_____

_____

_____

_____

_____

_____

_____

_____

_____

_____

But grow in grace, and in the knowledge of our Lord and Savior Jesus Christ. To Him be the glory both now and to the day of eternity. II Peter 3:18

*Iron sharpens iron, so a friend sharpens a friend.*
*Proverbs 27: 17 NLT*

Lord, help me to hear your voice today and always,
In Jesus name I pray. Amen

*Father, I stretch my hands to you, you are the only help I know. In Jesus name, Amen*

Dear God, I'm asking for you to guide my every thought and every word that comes out of my mouth today, in Jesus name I pray.   Amen

Precious Lord, watch over me as I lay down in my bed
tonight. In Jesus name Amen

_____

_____

_____

_____

_____

_____

_____

_____

_____

_____

_____

_____

_____

But thou, O LORD, art a shield for me; my glory, and
the lifter of mine head.  ~ Psalms 3: 3 KJV

*Give ear to my words, O LORD, consider my mediation.* ~Psalms 5: 1 KJV

Whoever does not love does not know God, because God is love. ~ 1 John 4:8 NIV

*Those who seek the Lord lack no good thing.*
*Psalms 34: 10 NIV*

*In all my prayers for all of you, I always pray with joy. ~ Philippians 1: 4 NIV*

For his anger lasts only a moment, but his favor
lasts a lifetime, weeping may remain for a night, but
rejoicing comes in the morning.  ~Psalms 30: 5 NIV

ANOINTED
# *PRAYERS*
## GOING DEEP
## 40 DAYS 40 NIGHTS OF PRAYER

~~~~~~~~PRAYER JOURNAL~~~~~~~~

P.M. Prayers

Sis.Lynn Ingram

*By this all men will know that you are my disciples, if you love one another.  ~ John 13: 35 NIV*

*I can do all things through Christ which strengtheneth me.* ~ *Philippians 4: 13 KJV*

_____

_____

_____

_____

_____

_____

_____

_____

_____

_____

_____

_____

_____

_____

_____

_____

But ye, beloved, building up yourselves up in your most holy faith, praying in the Holy Ghost.
~ Jude 1: 20 KJV

*O worship the LORD in the beauty of holiness: Fear before him, all thee earth.*
~ Psalms 96: 9 KJV

*And Jesus increased in wisdom and stature, and in favour with God and man. Luke 2: 52 KJV*

_____

_____

_____

_____

_____

_____

_____

_____

_____

_____

_____

_____

_____

_____

*He restoreth my soul: he leadeth me in the paths of righteousness for his name sake. ~ Psalms 23: 3 KJV*

---

---

---

---

---

---

---

---

---

---

---

---

---

---

---

---

*Worship the LORD your God, and his blessing will be on your food and water. I will take away sickness from among you,* ~Exodus 23: 25

_____

_____

_____

_____

_____

_____

_____

_____

_____

_____

_____

_____

_____

_____

*Blessed shalt thou be when thou come in, and blessed shalt thou be when thou goest out.*
*~ Deuteronomy 28: 6 KJV*

_____

_____

_____

_____

_____

_____

_____

_____

_____

_____

_____

_____

_____

_____

_____

*If any of you lacks wisdom, you should ask God, who gives generously to all without finding fault, and it will be given to you.* ~James 1: 5 NIV

---

_____

_____

_____

_____

_____

_____

_____

_____

_____

_____

_____

_____

_____

_____

*Prove by the way you live that you have repented of your sin and turned to God.* ~ Matthew 3: 8 NLT

*I will lift up mine eyes toward the hills, from whence cometh my help.*
*~ Psalms 121: 1 KJV*

---

---

---

---

---

---

---

---

---

---

---

---

---

*Mercy, peace and love be yours in abundance.*
*~ Jude 1: 2 NIV*

When hard pressed, I cried to the LORD; he brought me into a spacious place.  ~ Psalms 118: 5 NIV

_____

_____

_____

_____

_____

_____

_____

_____

_____

_____

_____

_____

_____

_____

This means that anyone who belongs to Christ has become a new person. The old life is gone; a new life has begun! ~ II Corinthians 5:17 NLT

Who satisfieth thy mouth with good things; so that
thy youth is renewed like the eagle's.
~ Psalms 103: 5 KJV

_____

_____

_____

_____

_____

_____

_____

_____

_____

_____

_____

_____

_____

_____

*It is by grace you have been saved.*
*~ Ephesians 2; 5b NIV*

*No, in all these things we are more than conquerors through him who loved us.* ~ Romans 8: 3 NIV

_____

_____

_____

_____

_____

_____

_____

_____

_____

_____

_____

_____

_____

_____

*I urge you, first of all, to pray for all people. Ask God to help them; intercede on their behalf, and give thanks for them.* ~1 Timothy 2: 1 NLT

*Love the Lord your God with all your heart and with all your soul and with all your mind and with all your strength.  ~Mark 12: 30 NIV*

_____

_____

_____

_____

_____

_____

_____

_____

_____

_____

_____

_____

_____

And the peace of God, which passeth all understanding, shall keep your hearts and minds through Christ Jesus.
~ Philippians 4: 7 KJV

*Pray without ceasing.* ~Thessalonians 5: 17 KJV

*Trust in the LORD with all your heart, and lean not on your own understanding; in all your ways acknowledge Him, and He shall direct your paths.*
*~ Proverbs 3: 5 NKJV*

*O magnify the Lord with me, and let us exalt his name together.* ~ Psalms 34: 3 KJV

---

---

---

---

---

---

---

---

---

---

---

---

---

---

*And my God shall supply all your needs according to His riches in glory by Christ Jesus.*
*~Philippians 4:19 NKJV*

For I will restore health to you and heal you of your wounds: says the LORD,  ~Jeremiah 30: 17a.

_____

_____

_____

_____

_____

_____

_____

_____

_____

_____

_____

_____

_____

_____

My covenant I will not break, nor alter the word that has gone out of My lips. ~Psalms 89: 34 NKJV

_____

_____

_____

_____

_____

_____

_____

_____

_____

_____

_____

_____

_____

_____

_____

*For all the promises of God in Him are Yes, and in Him Amen, to the glory of God through us.*
*~ II Corinthians 1: 20 NKJV*

_____

_____

_____

_____

_____

_____

_____

_____

_____

_____

_____

_____

_____

_____

*I love the LORD, for he heard my voice; he heard my cry for mercy.* ~ Psalms 116:1 NIV

And call upon me in the day of trouble:  I will deliver
thee, and thou shalt glorify me.  ~Psalms 50: 15 KJV

_____
_____
_____
_____
_____
_____
_____
_____
_____
_____
_____
_____
_____
_____

*He shall call upon me, and I will answer him: I will be with him in trouble; I will deliver him, and honour him.*
*~Psalms 91: 15 KJV*

*He hath made his wonderful works to be remembered: the LORD is gracious and full of compassion.* ~
PSALMS 111:4 KJV

*Thou shalt not be afraid for the terror by night, nor for the arrow that flieth by day; ~Psalms 91: 5 KJV*

*For He shall give his angels charge over thee, to keep thee in all thy ways. ~Psalms 91: 11 KJV*

*I will fear no evil, for you are with me.*
*~Psalms 23: 4 NIV*

*God is our refuge and strength, an ever-present help in trouble.* ~Psalms 46:1 NIV

_____

_____

_____

_____

_____

_____

_____

_____

_____

_____

_____

_____

_____

_____

*The Lord will fight for you, you need only to be still.*
*~ Exodus 14: 14 NIV*

*Cast all your anxiety in him because he cares for you.*
*~1 Peter 5: 7 NIV*

*If God is all you have, you have all you need.*
*~ John 14: 8 NIV*

---

---

---

---

---

---

---

---

---

---

---

---

---

---

---

*Cast your cares on the Lord and he will sustain you,
He will let the righteous fall.  ~Psalms 55: 22 NIV*

---

---

---

---

---

---

---

---

---

---

---

---

---

---

Now unto him that is able to keep you from falling, and to present you faultless before the presence of his glory with exceeding joy, To the only wise God our Saviour, be glory and majesty, dominion and power, both now and ever. Amen. ~Jude 1:24-25 KJV

_____

_____

_____

_____

_____

_____

_____

_____

_____

_____

_____

_____

_____

NOW THAT YOU HAVE READ 40 DAYS 40
NIGHTS, PRAYER JOURNAL. I KNOW
YOUR LIFE IS RENEWED, REFRESHED AND
REFILLED WITH GODS GLORY AND HIS
GOODNESS. CONTINUE TO PRAY AND
SEEK HIS FACE. STUDY HIS WORD TO
SHOW YOURSELF APPROVED. GREAT
THINGS ARE IN STORE FOR YOU. HIS
WORD SAYS: *BUT AS IT IS WRITTEN,
EYE HATH NOT SEEN, NOR EAR HEARD,
NIETHER HAVE ENTERED INTO THE
HEART OF MAN THE THINGS WHICH
GOD HATH PREPARED FOR THEM THAT
LOVE HIM. I CORINTHIANS 2: 9 KJV*

And he said unto me, My grace is sufficient for thee: for my strength is made perfect in weakness. Most gladly therefore will I rather glory in my infirmities, that the power of Christ may rest upon me.
~II Corinthians 12: 9

6b. 'NOT BY MIGHT NOR BY POWER, BUT BY MY SPIRIT, SAYS THE LORD ALMIGHTY.

~ZECHARIAH 4: 6b NIV

TO GOD BE THE GLORY FOR THE THINGS HE HAD DONE, AND THE THINGS HES DOING IN MY LIFE!

Sis. Lynn Ingram

But each day the LORD pours his unfailing love upon me, and through each night I sing his songs, praying to God who gives me life.

Psalms ~42: 8 NLT

*Sis. Lynn Ingram Is married to Maurice O. Ingram, a mother of six loving children and four wonderful grandchildren.*

*Sis. Lynn Ingram is member of New Mt. Zion Missionary Baptist Church, where the Rev. Dr. Jimmie T. Wafer is her pastor and Frist Lady Angela Wafer whom she loves dearly. ~Jeremiah 3:15*

*Sis. Lynn Ingram is an anointed prayer warrior who stays in the face of God.   ~Luke 21:36  / Ephesians 6:18 /  I Thessalonians 5:17*

*Sis. Lynn Ingram is a graduate of Geraldine Marvell Miller Wright Institute for Women In Ministry where Evangelist Elaine P. Wright is director/visionary.          ~II Timothy 2:15*

*Sis. Lynn Ingram is the president of the Prayer Ministry, she's instructor of the Liturgical Dance Ministry, Sis. Ingram is also the instructor of Flags of Fire and Women of Worship dance ministry.  Her passion is praying for all God's children, helping the elderly and attending to the sick.  ~Colossians 3:23*

*Sis. Ingram favorite scripture is Psalm 84:11 which were always quoted to her by the late Rev. Dr. James L. Newby III.  Lynn lives this quote "Only what you do for Christ will last!" her favorite song is… "Changed" By Walter Hawkins.*